AWKWARD!
Your Stars' OOPS, GOOFS & BLUSHES

by Michael-Anne Johns

SCHOLASTIC INC.

UNAUTHORIZED:

This book is not sponsored by or affiliated with any of the stars featured or with anyone involved with them.

© 2014 by Scholastic
ISBN 978-0-545-66838-5

Published by Scholastic Inc.
SCHOLASTIC and associated logos are trademarks and/or registered trademarks of Scholastic Inc.

10 9 8 7 6 5 4 3 2 1

14 15 16 17 18/0

Printed in the U.S.A.

40

First printing, September 2014

CONTENTS

INTRODUCTION

It's true—your favorite superstars live a life of glitz and glamour. They go to red-carpet events and wear gowns and tuxedos; they fly first class to exotic places all around the world, and they are photographed at fabulous parties and premieres.

But what about the times they're photographed tripping over a crack in the sidewalk? Or caught on mic saying something totally silly? The fact is, your favorite celebrities may be superstars, but they're ordinary people, too—people who make mistakes and find themselves in embarrassing situations like everyone else.

We've found some hysterical and unforgettable moments we just had to share. And the good thing is your fave stars are all such good sports, they're the ones who revealed these cringe-worthy tales.

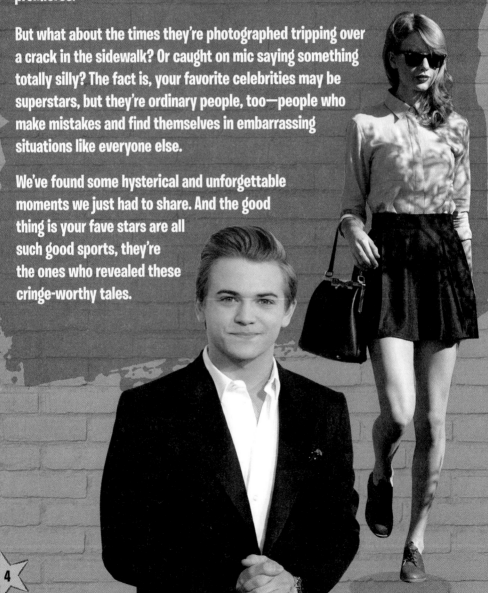

ONE DIRECTION

1D GUYS' TRAUMA-RAMAS!

They may be pop superstars, but Harry, Niall, Louis, Liam, and Zayn of 1D have had their real-life oops-moments, too. Here are the embarrassing memories they would like to forget!

HARRY STYLES . . . STOOD UP!

Oh, no! Harry turned bright red when Louis pulled his pants down in front of 20,000 fans at a 2013 concert at London's O2 Arena. But that wasn't the moment that makes Harry cringe most. That was when Harry was back in school in Holmes Chapel, England. "I was going out with a girl who lived next to a park with a little stream running through it," Harry told a *BOP* reporter. "So I bought loads of candles and laid them down. I called her and asked her to meet me. I'd been planning it *all* day, but she said she didn't want to come out. So I just stood there, kicking candles into the stream and getting kind of upset. It was probably one of the most embarrassing moments of my life!" Awww!

Name: Harry Edward Styles
Birthday: February 1, 1994
Birthplace: Holmes Chapel, Cheshire, England
First Job: When Harry was in high school, he worked part-time at a bakery in Holmes Chapel.

NIALL HORAN . . . PARTING PANTS!

Like pal Harry, Niall has had some wardrobe disasters of his own. One time he was playing golf with the British band Jack the Lad Swing's Marvin Humes. Later that day, Niall tweeted, "Just played golf with marv! Great laugh! I split my trousers right down the middle on the first hole, tie'n my shoe laces hahaha! #fool!" Oops!

Name: Niall James Horan
Birthday: September 13, 1993
Birthplace: Mullingar, County Westmeath, Ireland
Best Present: his first guitar

LOUIS TOMLINSON . . . MAMA'S BOY!

Louis and his mom have always been super close. His mom even posts pictures of him regularly on Twitter! But how does Louis feel about the fact that his fans regularly contact *his mom* on Twitter? "A lot of girls have contacted me [for] advice about boyfriends and help with their problems," his mom, Johanna, told *J-14.* "I try and answer as much as I can." Luckily for her, Louis doesn't seem to find this embarrassing. In fact, he tweets his mom regularly when he's on the road to let her know he misses her. Aw, what a guy!

Name: Louis William Tomlinson
Birthday: December 24, 1991
Birthplace: Doncaster, South Yorkshire, England
Favorite Early Job: hospitality suite waiter at the Doncaster Rovers soccer stadium

ZAYN MALIK . . . EXCUSE ME, PLEASE!

Zayn is a big dog lover. When 1D was in the U.S. for their 2013 tour, Zayn decided to get a new companion. So he went to a dog breeder and came back with nine-week-old Harley. Harley even rode in the tour bus with the guys. But that led to Zayn's uh-oh moment. Seems that Harley wasn't house-trained yet. "The boys love him, although he pooed on the bus [and] I wasn't there recently," he told *The Sun.* "It stunk it out and Louis stepped in it. He had socks on, but he really wasn't too happy." Who would be?!

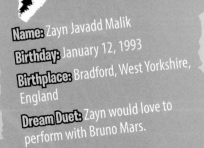

Name: Zayn Javadd Malik
Birthday: January 12, 1993
Birthplace: Bradford, West Yorkshire, England
Dream Duet: Zayn would love to perform with Bruno Mars.

LIAM PAYNE . . . SWEETHEART SERENADE!

Before Liam was in 1D, he once serenaded a girl he had a crush on. "I was young and naïve, and I'll never do that again," he told *Teen Vogue*. "I sang to her and asked her out. She went out with me once and dumped me. Sad story. It was really embarrassing!" What's worse is that he did it in school, with lots of his and her friends in earshot. ". . . I just broke into song like in *High School Musical*. I sang Mario's 'Let Me Love You.' How cheesy! It was probably the worst thing I ever did."

Name: Liam James Payne

Birthday: August 29, 1993

Birthplace: Wolverhampton, West Midlands, England

Favorite Sports: cross-country running and boxing

SELENA GOMEZ

Star of TV, film, and the concert stage, Selena, 22, was a typical teen. She experimented with fashion, her hair, and makeup. Sometimes it was a success, and sometimes it was a major oops!

MAKEUP DISASTER

Today it seems like actress and singer Selena always looks absolutely perfect. But that wasn't always so. When she was in school in her hometown of Grand Prairie, Texas, she decided to start wearing makeup. That turned out to be an embarrassing mistake. "I put tons of blue eye shadow on my finger, and wiped it all over my eyes," she told *BOP*. "I kept putting it on without realizing I looked like a clown! It was all over my face. This one guy came up to me and said, 'Why does your face look that way?' It was so awful!"

ALMOST FRIENDS

Even a superstar has awkward moments. When Selena met her favorite TV star at an awards ceremony, she didn't act cool, calm, and collected! "I ran away from Jennifer Aniston," Selena told *Glamour UK*. "When she said, 'hi,' I was terrified of her. I was scared, so I ran away and I'm really embarrassed about that. . . . I didn't know what to do. It's 'Rachel'!"

Name: Selena Marie Gomez

Birthday: July 22, 1992

Birthplace: Grand Prairie, Texas

Charity: Selena was named a UNICEF Ambassador in 2009—she is the youngest ever appointed.

Favorite Candy: Snickers and Good & Plenty

Showbiz Debut: Selena was a regular on *Barney & Friends* when she was seven years old.

11

ARIANA GRANDE

Star of Nickelodeon's *Sam & Cat*, Ariana showed a new side of her talent in 2013 when she released her debut album, *Yours Truly*. One music reviewer described it as "one of the best pop albums of the year." Of course, all her success doesn't make Ariana "oops-free"—check it out!

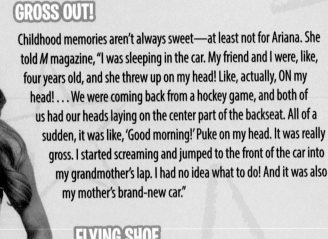

GROSS OUT!

Childhood memories aren't always sweet—at least not for Ariana. She told *M* magazine, "I was sleeping in the car. My friend and I were, like, four years old, and she threw up on my head! Like, actually, ON my head! . . . We were coming back from a hockey game, and both of us had our heads laying on the center part of the backseat. All of a sudden, it was like, 'Good morning!' Puke on my head. It was really gross. I started screaming and jumped to the front of the car into my grandmother's lap. I had no idea what to do! And it was also my mother's brand-new car."

FLYING SHOE

There are embarrassing moments in front of friends, and then there are the ones onstage in front of hundreds of people. Ariana knows! She recalled in an interview with Teen.com, "My most embarrassing moment onstage would probably be when I was doing *13* on Broadway, my shoe came off a few times. And I had to, like, work it into the choreography to go get it and pick it up and, like, dance with it. It was very weird. But it was fun, it worked out."

Name: Ariana Grande-Butera

Birthday: June 26, 1993

Birthplace: Boca Raton, Florida

Musical Influences: Mariah Carey, Whitney Houston, Fergie

Favorite Book Series: Harry Potter

Three Must-Haves on a Desert Island: rosewood lip gloss, her journal, and her cell phone

AUSTIN MAHONE

If you're a fan of Austin's, you are one of the millions of "Mahomies"! A down-to-earth kinda guy, Austin isn't afraid to share some of his most embarrassing moments.

SKINNY-DIPPING

Austin experienced a real "blusher moment" when he was a kid. "I was learning how to water-ski, and somehow my swim trunks, like, just came off," he told Scholastic's the STACKS Web site. "I don't know how it happened. They didn't rip. Like, my skis were on, so I don't know how it happened."

NOT SO ROSEY

Ask Austin about being humiliated in front of the girl he most wanted to impress, and he has a story to share! "We had this thing at school where you could buy roses, write your name on them, and they'd be sent to the person you wanted during class," he told *J-14*. "I bought the girl I had a crush on twelve roses, but a day went by and she still hadn't said anything about them to me. I thought it was weird, so finally, I was like, 'Did you get those roses?' She was like, 'What roses?' They never got delivered! I was like, 'Oh never mind. Forget I said anything.' I moved on and let it go."

Name: Austin Carter Mahone

Birthday: April 4, 1996

Birthplace: San Antonio, Texas

Socker-Man: Austin loves crazy socks and has more than 80 pairs!

Hidden Talent: He can wiggle his ears.

Favorite Animal: tiger

TAYLOR SWIFT

Taylor has come a long way from her days living with her family on an 11-acre Christmas tree farm in Pennsylvania. Even though her new home is at the top of the music charts, Taylor admits there have been times in her life she wished she could just fade into the background!

WRONG ROOM!

"[I was in an airport terminal and] the idea [for a song] came to me quickly, and I needed to write it down fast," she revealed to *J-14*. "The first thing I saw was a bathroom—and, well, there are paper towels in bathrooms, right?" Taylor ran in and jotted down some lyrics on a paper towel. "When I went back out to the terminal with part of my song on paper, I realized I had been inside the men's bathroom!"

NOT-SO-SECRET CRUSH

There are things you keep secret and things you share with friends, and Taylor learned the difference the hard way. "I was in the fifth grade, and these girls wanted me to tell them who I had a crush on," Taylor told *Yikes!* "I had never told anyone that I really liked the most popular guy in school, but I told them! Of course, they went right to the guy and told him what I'd said. It automatically turned into the most embarrassing thing ever. Everybody knew, and it was the most scarring week in fifth grade!"

Name: Taylor Alison Swift

Birthday: December 13, 1989

Birthplace: Reading, Pennsylvania

First Hobby: English-style horseback riding

Poetic Prowess: Taylor won a national poetry contest when she was in fourth grade. The poem was called "Monster in My Closet."

ROSS LYNCH

The *Austin & Ally* star and lead singer of R5, Ross Lynch also won the hearts of his fans as "Brady" in Disney Channel's *Teen Beach Movie*. In September 2013, R5 released their debut album, *Louder*. This heartthrob always seems so cool and collected, but he's the first to admit that's not always the case!

HAIR SCARE

There's nothing like a hair disaster, and Ross will never forget his! "My hairdresser cut my hair really short, and it was horrible," Ross told *BOP*. "It was cut straight across and kinda looked like a bowl. I'm pretty good at [calming myself down], but once my family and I got in the car, I totally freaked out!"

BRO PRANK

Ross remembers when his older brother pulled a first-day-of-school trick on him. "When I was younger, my brother told me that if I wanted to change classes, all I had to do was go into a new class and sit down," he laughingly recalled to *Twist*. "So one day I tried it. When I walked in, my friends called me over to sit down, but the teacher was like, 'No way, go back to your class!' I was so embarrassed. It was funny, but awkward!"

Name: Ross Shor Lynch

Birthday: December 29, 1995

Birthplace: Littleton, Colorado

Fun Fact: Ross and his siblings—Riker, Rydel, Rocky, and Ryland—are cousins of actress Julianne Hough and her *Dancing With the Stars* brother, Derek.

Yogurt Buddies: Ross appeared with Bella Thorne in a 2013 Danimals yogurt commercial.

Flying High: Ross wants to get his pilot's license someday.

DEBBY RYAN

Fans first met Debby on Disney Channel's *The Suite Life on Deck*. She went on to star in the channel's TV movies *16 Wishes* and *Radio Rebel*. She now stars on the Disney sitcom, *Jessie*. Debby loves a giggle, even when she has to laugh at herself!

CLUMSY DEBBY

Sometimes a dream day turns into a nightmare. Just check with Debby! "On Fourth of July, my friend and I were at Disneyland," Debby told Scholastic magazines. "We were the last ones there and as we were leaving, I tripped up the down escalator and tore my knee open. We ran around at one A.M. trying to find an emergency room. I was bleeding everywhere and the only thing we had to stop the bleeding was a Kleenex and a sock I found in the car. My friend also faints at the sight of blood, so things were a little dicey. We finally made it to the hospital. They stitched me up, and in the process they hooked my friend up to an IV so that she wouldn't pass out!"

IPOD CONFESSION

What does your iPod playlist say about you? According to Debby, sometimes it's not exactly what you want it to say! "The most embarrassing thing on my iPod?" she told *Entertainment Weekly*. "I do have an adequate amount of Phil Collins and a little bit of . . . I actually have a lot of movie scores. I listen to a lot of movie scores. For instance, the score of *Amélie*, the French film with Audrey Tautou, is possibly the best!"

Name: Deborah Ann Ryan

Birthday: May 13, 1993

Birthplace: Huntsville, Alabama

Favorite Food: chicken noodle soup

Pet: toy poodle named Presley, named after rock star Elvis Presley

Favorite Thing: Debby loves shoes— she has a massive collection.

CODY SIMPSON

Australian Cody Simpson is not only a talented singer but also a competitive swimmer and surfer. But Cody is most at home on a stage, performing for thousands of fans. He released his most recent album, *Surfer's Paradise*, in 2013. He may be a superstar, but Cody faces everyday mishaps just like everyone else!

POPCORN EXPLOSION

Cody knows what it's like to make a bad impression on a first date—just ask him about it! "I spilled popcorn all over both of us! I was just really clumsy . . . and I was nervous. It was a first date but luckily she was really relaxed and had a great sense of humor," he confessed to *Popstar!*

DON'T GO, MOMMY!

Admitting you're a mama's boy is embarrassing enough, but Cody took it to the limit! "When I was younger, I never wanted to leave my mom!" Cody revealed in *Twist*. "Every first day of school, I'd just cry. I'd hold on to her and rip her shirt to try not to leave her! Mom would get upset because I was hysterical, and it was horrible. I still remember it!"

Name: Cody Robert Simpson

Birthday: January 11, 1997

Birthplace: Gold Coast, Queensland, Australia

Chicken Song: Cody got his first guitar when he was seven years old and he then wrote his first song, which was about chickens.

Favorite Fruit: pineapple

Family Nickname: "Codes"

BLUSH-A-THON

See how some of your favorite stars handle their oops, goofs, and blushes!

OLIVIA HOLT (ACTRESS AND SINGER)

"I [was] in New York and I went to visit the Empire State Building," Oliva told Scholastic magazines. "We went up to the top and took pictures . . . [When] we were coming down in the elevator, I had my phone with me and I [was] taking a video. I started the video with the back of the elevator . . . and I turned [my phone] to me and said, 'Yes! That is the Eiffel Tower!' Everyone in the elevator just looked at me like, 'Did you just say the Eiffel Tower?' . . . It was very embarrassing!"

ASHLEY BENSON (ACTRESS AND MODEL)

"I was out to dinner at a sushi restaurant with one of my guy friends and I went to take a bite of my sushi only to realize I can't fit the whole roll in my mouth," she revealed to *Popstar!* "I was trying to bite it in half but th seaweed would not rip! So I'm trying to carry on a conversation and this sushi is just unrolling and making a complete mess!"

CONOR MAYNARD (SINGER-SONGWRITER)

"Meeting Rihanna was one of the most embarrassing moments of my life," he confessed to heatworld.com. "I had no idea I was going to meet her. I was on a plane coming back from L.A. to London and I didn't realize Rihanna was also on the plane. Someone tapped me on the shoulder when I was in my seat and it was Rihanna. She said, 'Congratulations on everything!' And I said, 'Ah . . . eh . . .'—that's literally all I could get out. A squeak. She's probably not a fan anymore."

CHINA ANNE MCCLAIN
(ACTRESS AND SINGER-SONGWRITER)

"I was working on a group project in class with my friends and I started talking about how much I liked my crush—talking about boys was way more fun than working on the project!" she told *Twist*. "I was telling them how much I liked him. . . . Then, I looked up and saw he was standing right by our table. He heard the whole thing! I was really embarrassed about it, but it actually helped break the ice. I think he was flattered to hear I liked him. But it was still super embarrassing."

JESSICA SANCHEZ (SINGER)

"I was in art class, and everyone was busy working, so it was super quiet," she revealed to *Seventeen*. "Suddenly my phone started blasting Soulja Boy's 'Tell 'Em' [sic] really loudly—I'd forgotten to turn off my ringer! The whole class was cracking up, like, 'Really, that's your ringtone?!?' I never forgot to turn off my phone after that!"

DYLAN SPRAYBERRY (ACTOR)

"I was at a friend's barbecue," he told *Girls' Life*. "There were a bunch of girls, so I tried to show off with a front flip into the pool. I overdid it and belly flopped so hard it knocked the breath out of me. I was hoping no one noticed, but when I made my way to the surface, everyone was laughing and cheering!"

VICTORIA JUSTICE
(ACTRESS AND SINGER-SONGWRITER)

"I was walking after school when a bird flew really close to my head," Victoria told Scholastic magazines. "I freaked out and started running and screaming. Everyone just turned around and started laughing . . . it was actually pretty funny."

CARLOS PENA, JR.
(ACTOR AND SINGER-SONGWRITER)

"I asked this girl out on a date, and I went to fill up the car at the gas station," he told *Yikes!* "[Then] I took her to this nice place, and the bill comes out and it's, like, a hundred bucks. I'm like, 'I got you, girl.'" But when Carlos reached for his wallet, it wasn't there! "Either I had left it somewhere at the gas station or dropped it somewhere. I didn't know where it was! So I was like, 'Hey, can you get this one and I'll get the next few? It was so awkward. It was one of the most embarrassing things I've ever been through!"

CALUM WORTHY (ACTOR)

"I'm pretty much the king of [embarrassing] stories," he kidded with Scholastic magazines. "I often have to wear a lot of crazy outfits on set that involve some special effect. Recently I had to be in this really large outfit. . . . There was this girl on set, somebody's guest, who was flirting with me and I'm trying to act all cool. I put my arm down and knock over the entire set and everything comes crashing down. I didn't get the date!"

RAINI RODRIGUEZ (ACTRESS AND SINGER)

"[When] we filmed our Christmas episode, I tripped on the staircase in the Sonic Boom [the music store on the *Austin & Ally* set] and I cut my arm," she admitted to Scholastic magazines. "It was a minor thing and they put a Band-Aid on it, but it kept coming off, so we wrapped my arm in gauze, which made it look like I had a cast on my arm, which made it look way worse than it was. That was [on a] Tuesday. On [that] Wednesday, I walked headfirst into a snowflake that was hanging on the wall and got a nice unicorn bump on my forehead. Pretty embarrassing!"

LAURA MARANO (ACTRESS AND SINGER)

"I have so many [embarrassing stories]!" she told Scholastic magazines. "Ross [Lynch] and I were filming this PSA [public service announcement] for Friends for Change two years ago. [It was] in this really beautiful forest area in California, and we were running and jumping on this log. Ross jumps perfectly and then I jump and fall right on my face, on the ground. Everyone was like, 'Laura, are you okay?' and I said, 'Yeah, I'm fine, let's do it again.' They were like, 'We're never letting you do it again!' It was so embarrassing!"

SABRINA CARPENTER (ACTRESS AND SINGER)

"Embarrassing moments?" Sabrina confided to Scholastic magazines. "Let me think. I was kind of, like, a joker in class, so I remember raising my hand a lot and instead of giving serious answers, I would make a joke and then I would get really embarrassed because my teachers would get mad at me. But I was always just kind of a happier person trying to lighten up the group."

ZENDAYA COLEMAN

Best known for her role as "Rocky Blue" on Disney Channel's *Shake It Up*, Zendaya dazzled the audience when she appeared on *Dancing With the Stars*. She released her debut album, *Zendaya*, on September 17, 2013. Of course, her success didn't protect her from these embarrassing moments!

PEEK-A-BOO

Sometimes a cool breeze is the last thing you need! "My pants ripped once when I was doing a *Shake It Up* photo shoot and I was doing these jumping poses," she told *Seventeen*. "I did one and felt a slight breeze in my backside. It was a little teeny rip, so I was like, 'Know what? We're fine. Nobody is going to see it. It's in the back. Whatever.' I did another picture and my jeans ripped in half! There were two separate pant legs. They showed me the picture after and you can see the pieces of thread flying in the air. It was mortifying!"

TOOTH TERROR

"My tooth stuck out! . . . When I was little, my teeth were pretty straight. But as I got older, one tooth shifted a bit," Zendaya told *Yikes!*, recalling one of her childhood "traumas." She even stopped smiling! So her parents decided to bring her to the dentist. "I was worried 'cause I'd never had braces, so I didn't know how it worked. But when I went, the orthodontist was nice, and I had nothing to worry about."

Name: Zendaya Coleman

Birthday: September 1, 1996

Birthplace: Oakland, California

Cool Fact: *Zendaya* means "to give thanks" in the Zimbabwean language of Shona.

Sundae Dream: "Häagen-Dazs ice cream. Three flavors: coffee, chocolate, mint chip. Topped with chocolate chips, chocolate, caramel syrup, and lots of whipped cream," Zendaya described to *BOP*.

Awesome Author: Zendaya wrote the book *Between U and Me: How to Rock Your Tween Years With Style and Confidence.*

DEMI LOVATO

Demi Lovato got her start back home in Texas on TV's *Barney & Friends*. As a teen, her big break was on Disney Channel's *Sonny With A Chance*. Demi is best known now as a singer: She released her fourth album, *Demi*, in May 2013. With such success, you might think she never gets embarrassed. Well, you'd be very wrong!

COFFEE RUN

Sometimes the best of times turn into the worst of times! Demi learned that when she was a teen and had gone on a coffee date with her latest crush. "I'm sitting there and I go to make a pinkie promise—I make those all the time—and when I do that, it flips my coffee into my lap," she told *J-14*. "The entire Starbucks cup flipped over, and it was completely full. I ran to the bathroom. At first I just sat there like, 'This is awkward.' . . . I was like . . . 'This is so embarrassing!'"

SCHOOL DAZE

When Demi was in sixth grade back at Cross Timbers Middle School in Grapevine, Texas, she had another blusher over a crush. One day she was telling her friends about how much she liked this boy, and her teacher happened to overhear her gushing away. "I had a crush on the most popular guy in the eighth grade," she told *BOP*. "Everyone was teasing me because I liked him. My teacher pulled him into the classroom and asked him, 'Did you know someone in this class has a HUGE crush on you?'"

Name: Demetria Devonne Lovato

Birthday: August 20, 1992

Birthplace: Albuquerque, New Mexico

Cool Fact: Demi used to be a vegetarian.

Piano Princess: Demi began to play the piano when she was seven years old.

Listen Up: Demi was the spokesperson for the anti-bullying organization, PACER.

JENNETTE MCCURDY

The costar of Nickelodeon's *iCarly* and *Sam & Cat*, Jennette started acting when she was five years old, and she hasn't stopped since! She also released her first album, *Jennette McCurdy*, in 2012. Known for her sense of humor, Jennette claims that her real life is like a sitcom!

DANCE-A-BOMB

"I was at an audition when I first started acting," she told Scholastic magazines. "I had just started dancing two weeks [before] and this was a dance audition. I had to go in and perform a dance in front of Paula Abdul. About five girls went in at a time and they [were] all awesome. You could see they had years of training. They were really impressive and I did my little dance. I did the two moves that I had learned. It was so terrible, but Paula was bobbing her head and trying to get into it. I promised myself then that I would really get into dancing and try to be good at it and never embarrass myself again."

MOMMA MIA

"My mom does a lot of embarrassing things," Jennette revealed to *J-14*. "You know that James Brown song, 'I Feel Good'? We were at Blockbuster, and she was doing this whole James Brown dance. She was doing the foot moves and everything. The entire staff was staring at her. It was very embarrassing."

Name: Jennette Michelle Faye McCurdy

Birthday: June 26, 1992

Birthplace: Long Beach, California

Favorite Food: sushi

Tweety: Jennette's first tweet was "My first tweet!"

First Celebrity Crush: Johnny Depp

33

BELLA THORNE

The *Shake It Up* star has appeared in more than 20 films and TV series. Bella has also filmed dozens of commercials, but now she is concentrating on her music career. Her debut album is due out in 2014. Always willing to share the good and the bad, Bella hopes fans can relate to some of her red-faced moments!

LUNCH BREAK

"I think I have embarrassing moments every day—24/7," she told Celebuzz.com. "A good one though was on set. It was lunch, and I was talking to Adam [Irigoyen]—everybody's usually in my room at lunch or Davis [Cleveland]'s room, and in my room—the whole cast was there, and I was talking to Adam and I was like, 'Yeah' and I walked right into a wall, smack dab in the middle of my face. It was hilarious, and Adam was like, 'Wow, Bella, way to be smart!' and he did the same exact thing."

WRONG DOOR

Bella told *J-14*, "I was at a restaurant and the [bathroom] doors didn't have signs on them for girls and guys." Bella chose one and when she was washing her hands, a guy was at the sink. "I looked at him like, 'Eww, sicko! What are you doing in the girls' bathroom?' But then I turned around and saw the urinals. I was like, 'Oops!' and ran out of there so fast!"

Name: Annabella Avery Thorne

Birthday: October 8, 1997

Birthplace: Pembroke Pines, Florida

Favorite Disneyland Ride: Space Mountain

Princess: Bella was named after "Belle" from *Beauty and the Beast.*

First Language: Spanish—her late father was Cuban.

DREW CHADWICK

Emblem3 made their first national appearance on the U.S. version of *The X Factor*. They are brothers Wesley and Keaton Stromberg, and friend Drew Chadwick. They came in fourth on the second season of the show, but signed a deal with Simon Cowell's label, Syco Music, and Columbia Records. Their first album, *Nothing to Lose*, was released in 2013. Drew is often the spokesman for the fun-loving group, so he shares some of his most embarrassing memories.

BLUSH-A-MOM

"[My mom] rolled up to our concert wearing giant granny panties over her pants once! I was like, 'No! Leave!'" Drew told *J-14*.

NAME GAME

"At one of our concerts I announced [a friend's] birthday onstage and got his name wrong!" he told Hollywire.com. "I said, 'My friend, Gary! Get up, Gary!'...'It's Greg! It's Greg!' everyone onstage was saying! Embarrassing!"

Name: Drew Michael Chadwick

Birthday: October 1, 1992

Birthplace: Port Angeles, Washington

Poetic Prowess: Drew is a published poet.

Instruments: guitar, ukulele, piano

Passion: Drew is an environmentalist.

FIFTH HARMONY

Ally Brooke, Dinah Hansen, Lauren Jauregui, Normani Kordei, and Camila Cabello became a singing group, Fifth Harmony, when they auditioned as solo acts on the second season of *The X Factor*. They were teamed up as a group and placed third in the competition, but they signed a deal with Syco Music and Epic Records soon after. Besides talent, the girls share a great sense of humor and the honesty to admit they sometimes make laughable mistakes!

DONUTS TO GO FOR DINAH!

Dinah: "My mom signed me up [to audition for *The X Factor*]," she told *Teen Vogue*. "It was last minute, so when I got through the judges' round I had to fly from L.A. to Rhode Island, because that was the last stop. I ended up auditioning on my birthday! I was kind of scared because they told us to go to the Dunkin' Donuts Center, and I didn't realize that was actually the stadium where auditions were happening. I thought they meant an actual donut shop, so I thought the whole thing wasn't for real!"

PANTSED

The fivesome told *Pacific Rim Video Press*:
Dinah: "We were in the dressing room and Camila puts both her feet in one pants leg! So she falls over and she's still in her underpants. And one of the wardrobe ladies . . . she fell on one of the wardrobe ladies' face!"
Camila: "I was facedown!"

CLOSET NIGHTMARES

The harmonizers told *Twist* about some fashion mishaps:
Lauren: "I went through a really intense poncho phase in elementary school. I remember we were playing Truth or Dare at lunch, and this guy made me eat something really disgusting. That's when I threw up on the poncho! So I haven't worn it since!"
Ally: "I have a mariachi outfit. When I was little, like six or something, I was singing somewhere and I had to wear it!"
Normani: "I have a Cheetah Girls outfit—I think I wore it for Halloween."

Name: Allyson Brooke Hernandez
Birthday: July 7, 1993
Birthplace: San Antonio, Texas
Favorite Movie: *Titanic*
Brotherly Love: Her brother named her Ally after the character "Ali" in *The Karate Kid.*
Celebrity Crush: Ed Sheeran

Name: Normani Kordei Hamilton
Birthday: May 31, 1996
Birthplace: Atlanta, Georgia
Favorite Pastimes: playing video games and shopping
Favorite Activities: gymnastics and dancing
Early Goal: to be an Olympic gymnast

Name: Lauren Michelle Jauregui
Birthday: June 27, 1996
Birthplace: Miami, Florida
Favorite Food: Nutella
Celebrity Crush: Zayn Malik
Land of the Brave: Lauren sang the national anthem in front of her whole school when she was in the fifth grade.

Name: Karla Camila Cabello
Birthday: March 3, 1997
Birthplace: Cojimar, Cuba
Favorite Singer: Demi Lovato
Favorite Food: bananas
Favorite Superhero: Spider-Man

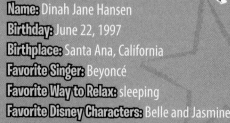

Name: Dinah Jane Hansen
Birthday: June 22, 1997
Birthplace: Santa Ana, California
Favorite Singer: Beyoncé
Favorite Way to Relax: sleeping
Favorite Disney Characters: Belle and Jasmine

RICO RODRIGUEZ

The laugh-a-minute Rico Rodriguez is pretty much the opposite of his *Modern Family* character, "Manny Delgado," who is serious and not so carefree. But that's why Rico loves playing Manny—he gets to play a totally different person. While Manny would be crushed by an embarrassing situation, Rico just takes it in stride and moves on!

I NEED MY MOMMY

"[When I went on my first audition], I wanted my mom to go in the room with me," Rico recalled in an interview with Backstage.com. "She was like, 'Rico, you're supposed to go in and do things by yourself.' I was like, 'What!' Nobody had told me *that*."

MOMMY NUMBER TWO

"At first I had a little mom crush on her [costar Sofia Vergara]," he revealed to Hollywoodlife.com. "[But then] I thought that would be so weird because I work with her every day and she's like a real mom to me and it would be weird if I had a crush on my mom. So I was like, 'I'm just gonna scratch that!'"

Name: Rico Rodriguez

Birthday: July 31, 1998

Birthplace: College Station, Texas

Fun Fact: Rico and "Manny" do share one hobby—they both love to cook.

Hidden Talent: He's an amateur magician.

Favorite Candy: Sour Patch Kids

HUNTER HAYES

By the time he was seven, Hunter had appeared on national TV shows and was invited to perform for President Bill Clinton at the White House. Luckily, Hunter didn't have any embarrassing moments there! But he's had other blusher moments.

FIGURE IT OUT VIDEOS

"Embarrassing. I mean, it's awkward!" Hunter told JustJaredJr.com. about when his parents show clips of his first TV work on the show *Figure It Out*. "It's like you have friends over, and Mom and Dad point out the baby pictures. You just want to run out of the room for a second. . . . It's very bizarre. I can't believe I was lucky enough to find music that early in my life."

MR. CLEAN

It's embarrassing when people find out Hunter's secret obsession. He told *Twist*, "I'm secretly a bit compulsive about my space! It's often a complete mess, in which case, I'm absolutely wrecked as soon as I walk in. If I come back and it's cluttered, I have to spend thirty minutes cleaning up so I can live in there for the rest of the night!"

Name: Hunter Easton Hayes

Birthday: September 9, 1991

Birthplace: Breaux Bridge, St. Martin Parish, Louisiana

Fun Fact: Hunter played accordion and sang onstage with country music legend Hank Williams Jr. when he was just four years old.

Instruments: accordion, guitar, bass guitar, drums, and keyboard, to name a few—he can play more than 30!

Fearsome Fans: Hunter's fans are called "Hayniacs."

PEYTON LIST

Peyton Roi List has been performing since she was four years old. Her biggest films have been *The Sorcerer's Apprentice*, *Diary of a Wimpy Kid: Rodrick Rules*, and *Diary of a Wimpy Kid: Dog Days*. But most fans know her as "Emma" from Disney Channel's sitcom, *Jessie*. Judging by her embarrassing moments, Peyton's life could be a comedy!

SKIRT ATTACK!

"A couple of years ago I remember I really, really wanted to wear this skirt, but it was way too big for me," Peyton told *Twist*. "So I asked my mom to pin it up for me. Later, I was walking down the street with my mom and my brothers and all of a sudden, my skirt just fell to my ankles! I remember being so embarrassed. I looked around—luckily there weren't a lot of people around, so I just pulled it back up and kept on walking. But it was still so embarrassing!"

CAN YOU SEE THIS?

"I went to an eye appointment . . . and had to get my pupils dilated," she told *Seventeen*. "The doctor said my eyes would be sensitive to light for the next six or seven hours and handed me these glasses that would protect them. They looked like they were made for an old man! On the way home with my mom, we stopped at a coffee shop and my crush was there. I wanted to whip off the ugly glasses so badly, but my mom wouldn't let me. Of course, he came over to talk to me and I was completely mortified!"

Name: Peyton Roi List

Birthday: April 6, 1998

Birthplace: Florida

Siblings: Peyton has a twin brother, Spencer, and younger brother, Phoenix.

Nickname: "Pey"

Cover Girl: Peyton appeared on the cover of *American Girl's* 2008 back-to-school issue.

OOPS-WORTHY SLIPS OF THE TONGUE

Remember when you were just learning to speak? Some words were very hard to pronounce. It's all part of growing up, and your favorite celebrities had those moments, too. Years later it might seem embarrassing, but really, it was just cute! Check out what they told Scholastic magazines!

BELLA THORNE (ACTRESS)

"*Specific*—I still have a problem with this word I can't say. It's se . . . sespi . . . I can't say it! It just doesn't come out. It's spe-ci-fic . . . sespific. *Noooo!*"

DEBBY RYAN (ACTRESS)

"I couldn't say my *r*'s until I was eleven years old. I was 'Debwa.' . . . Oh, and *yellow* was 'lellow.' I couldn't say yellow."

JENNETTE MCCURDY (ACTRESS)

"Whenever someone said, 'I must do this,' I thought they were saying 'I mustard this.'"

LAURA MARANO (ACTRESS)

"I used to have trouble with my *r*'s . . . I would put a *w* instead of an *r*, which I thought was hilarious. But it's funny . . . Now I say my *r*'s correctly, but I can't roll my *r*'s. . . . I literally cannot make my tongue roll!"

CYMPHONIQUE (ACTRESS AND SINGER)

"*Hmmm*. I think *water* was the hardest word. I used to say it like *wahduh*. And for *warm*, I would say *wum*."

CONOR MAYNARD (SINGER-SONGWRITER)

"The word was *music*. I used to say *zic*. There's a funny story behind that. My mom knew what I meant when I said it. I'd go 'Zic on. Zic on,' and I meant I wanted to hear music. Once my auntie was looking after me, and I was going, 'Zic on. Zic on.' She thought I was going to be sick. So she called my mom to come pick me up. . . . When my mom got there, she was like, 'No, he just wants to listen to music.'"

BLAKE MICHAEL (ACTOR)

"*Chair* was my hardest word. I would always say *share*. I couldn't do the *ch-* sound."

ROSHON FEGAN (ACTOR)

"*Cadillac*. I used to say *cataracts*. I used to say, 'Dad, when I grow up, I want a cataract', and he would say, 'Oh, no you don't, son; no, you don't.'"

MAIA MITCHELL (ACTRESS)

"*Cucumber*. I used to say *cucombombom*. I could never get it and I was, like, seven years old."

MADISON PETTIS (ACTRESS)

"*Chick-fil-A* was really hard for me to pronounce. I love Chick-fil-A, but I would always say *Chick-fey-A*."

CAROLINE SUNSHINE (ACTRESS)

"The word *specific* was really hard for me. . . . . I would say, 'Can you be more pacific about it?' I didn't know how to say the *sp-*."

JOSH HUTCHERSON (ACTOR)

"My brother and I both said *pasghetti* instead of *spaghetti*."

CHINA ANNE MCCLAIN (ACTRESS AND SINGER-SONGWRITER)

"When I was five, I could never pronounce the word *probably*. I would always end up saying *pro-bubbly*!"

ZENDAYA COLEMAN (ACTRESS AND SINGER)

"*Milk*. I would say *mouk*. I don't know why I couldn't say the *–lk*, and so I would say, 'Can I get some chocolate mouk?'"

CODY SIMPSON (SINGER)

"I used to say *musmus* instead of *Christmas*."

LEO HOWARD (ACTOR)

"*Banana*—I pronounced it *nana*. But I was obsessed with that word. It was the first word that I ever learned and I was talking about bananas and every time I'd see it in a store, I would go, 'Nana! Nana!' I would go crazy screaming 'nana' and my parents had to hide the bananas in [the] house."